"Ready to Give a Defense"

Answering Our Friends' Religious Questions

By Kyle Pope

truth
BOOKS

ISBN 10: 1-58427-386-0
ISBN 13: 978-158427-386-8

Guardian of Truth Foundation
CEI Bookstore
220 S. Marion St
Athens, Alabama 35611
1-855-49-BOOKS or 1-855-492-6657
www.CEIbooks.com

Preface

James declared through the Holy Spirit, **"he who turns a sinner from the error of his way will save a soul from death"** (James 5:20). Solomon echoed the similar thought, **"he who wins souls is wise"** (Prov. 11:30). There is nothing one can do in this life that demonstrates love for another person more than trying to teach that person the truth. The question is how do we do this? What do we say? How do we answer questions that arise? Christians must prepare themselves to be ready to act when opportunities arise.

The material in this study was first prepared for a series of home Bible studies in Amarillo, Texas at the request of young adults seeking to prepare themselves for just such opportunities. Later the same material was used in adult classes at the Olsen Park church of Christ in Amarillo. These lessons are intended to help prepare Christians to answer common questions that arise when talking to our friends. Thirteen basic areas are addressed, after first considering the goal and disposition that should govern all such discussions.

These lessons will not give you a script of rehearsed answers, but they will lay a foundation to enable you to respond to some of the main questions you may face. We must understand that it is the word of God that converts souls (Rom. 1:16; James 1:18; Psa. 19:7). We must bring people to Scripture in the assurance that God's word will accomplish its objective (Isa. 55:11). It is my hope that this material proves helpful in your work to teach your friends. May God bless your efforts to teach the gospel to lost souls.

Kyle Pope
February 2013

Table of Contents

Lesson One
Attitudes and Objectives

Read: **1 Peter 3:12-16.** Peter urges Christians, through the Holy Spirit, to be **"ready to give a defense for the hope"** that lay within them. Jesus taught that those who follow Him must let their light **"shine before men"** so the world will see us and glorify God (Matt. 5:16). The apostles were charged to **"make disciples of all the nations"** (Matt. 28:19-20). Christians today must carry on this work as we work to teach our friends, neighbors, and family. In this lesson we will consider the proper attitudes and objectives we should have in carrying out this task.

I. Our Attitude toward Teaching Our Friends.

A. What is our attitude toward ourselves as we teach our friends?

    1. **"First remove the plank from your own eye"** (Luke 6:41-42). Jesus teaches in this text that we can only see accurately to help others come to the truth when we are first willing to look at our own shortcomings. If we fail to do this we can come across to others as arrogant or self-righteous. Jesus warned that the one who approaches God self-righteously is not acceptable to Him (Luke 18:9-14). Further, if we have sin in our lives it can damage our credibility with our friends. We must show our friends that gratitude to God for His mercy motivates our desire to teach them.

> Sin I ignore in my own life hurts my relationship to God and damages my credibility.

B. What is our attitude toward our friends as we teach them?

    1. **"Making a distinction"** (Jude 22-23). Jude, through the Holy Spirit instructed two distinct ways to approach teaching others. *First,* **"On some have compassion,"** but *Second,* **"others save with fear, pulling them out of the fire, hating even the garment defiled**

Attitudes and Objectives

by the flesh." Jesus displayed this distinction in His teaching. He was very sharp and firm in His rebuke of the stubborn self-righteous attitudes of the Pharisees (Matt. 23:29-33), but gentle and compassionate to souls ignorant of the truth (John 4:19-24) or broken-hearted over their own sin (Luke 7:37-47). In teaching others we must seek to make this same distinction. While some will only be moved by a sharp rebuke, others are ignorant of the truth and require honest, gentle, and compassionate instruction.

2. **"I still have many things to say to you, but you cannot bear them now"** (John 16:12). Jesus recognized when teaching His apostles that they could not receive everything they needed to learn about the gospel at one time. Often in trying to teach someone we feel as if we must give them everything the Bible teaches on an issue all at once. While we should never be afraid to declare the **"whole counsel of God"** (Acts 20:27), we must recognize that people are limited in what they can absorb in one sitting. Sometimes, planting the seed and giving it time to germinate and grow is the very thing that is needed.

> We can't teach everything all at once—people can only learn so much at one time.

II. The Objective of Teaching Our Friends.

A. What is our goal in teaching our friends?

1. **"The end of your faith—the salvation of your souls"** (1 Pet. 1:6-9). The goal of faith and thus the goal of evangelism is the salvation of the soul. It is not winning an argument. It is not self-exaltation. It is leading the soul of a person who is lost in sin out of the perilous condition of eternal condemnation into a saving relationship with God. The goal is leading that soul unto eternal life in the age to come. We must keep this objective in our minds in all that we say and do in teaching the lost.

B. The Problem of Sin.

1. **"All have sinned and fall short of the glory of God"** (Rom. 3:23). A good starting point in talking with our friends is to focus on the problem of sin. The reason Jesus died was because of our sin. The reason people will be lost is sin. The reason all human beings need salvation is sin. The reason that it is important to act

within the authority of Scripture is because the failure to do so is sin.

2. "Sin is lawlessness" (1 John 3:4-8). To understand the problem of sin we must first understand how sin is defined. Sin is not just feeling bad about something. We might feel bad about things that don't matter to God. Sin is not just making someone else feel bad. Sometimes people may want things that God does not. Sin is the violation of God's law. In this age God's law is embodied in the New Covenant or **"Law of Christ"** (Gal. 6:1,2). All people everywhere are accountable to this Law (1 Cor. 9:19-22).

3. "To him who knows to do good and does not do it, to him it is sin" (James 4:17). Sin not only involves doing things that God prohibits but failing to do what God commands us to do. This is true whether we are talking about personal conduct, how we treat our families, how we behave at work, or how we worship God. Until we can lead someone to recognize that doing what is unauthorized is sin, a careful study of what the Bible teaches in these areas means very little to a person.

> We must help our friends understand that sin condemns us before God.

Conclusion.

There is nothing that demonstrates love for another person more than seeking to teach them the truth. We must be diligent to do this whenever we have the opportunity. Our love can lead souls to be saved and cause the kingdom of our Lord to grow.

Study Questions.

1. The word translated "defense" in 1 Peter 3:15 is the Greek word *apologia* (ἀπολογία). Some Christians in the first centuries after Christ wrote texts called *apologies* in which they explained and

Attitudes and Objectives

defended their belief in Jesus to unbelievers. What are some things a Christian should be prepared to explain if we are "ready to give a defense"? _____

_____

_____

2. In Luke 6:41-42, when Jesus taught about judging a "speck" in someone else's eye while we have a "plank" in our own eye, is He teaching that it is best not to even try and teach someone the truth? _____

_____

_____

3. What does Paul teach in 1 Corinthians 8:1 about the danger of arrogant knowledge? How can this relate to our efforts to teach others the truth? _____

_____

_____

4. Explain the difference between Jude's teaching on making a "distinction" and showing "partiality" or "respect of persons" condemned in James 2:1-9? How may we practice the one and avoid the other? _____

_____

_____

5. What is the context of Jesus' teaching in John 16:12 and what did He promise to send them since they could not "bear" learning all they needed to at that time? _____

_____

_____

6. What are some ways that our world has led people to feel guilty for things that are not sinful, but tolerant of things that are? _____

_____

_____

7. How does James 4:17 indicate the importance of making certain that all that we do in worshipping God be done with the Divine authority?

_____

_____

Lesson Two
Authority in Religion

Introduction.

hile Jesus was upon the earth He was asked a very important question by the Jewish leaders—**"by what authority do you do these things?"** Jesus responded to the question with His own question. He asked them if the teaching of John the Baptist came **"from heaven or from men?"** (Matt. 21:23-27). When the Jewish leaders refused to answer Him, Jesus refused to answer their question. Since they would not acknowledge the obvious fact that John's message came from heaven, Jesus refused to directly acknowledge that His own message also came from heaven. In this exchange Jesus showed by His question that religious authority is either derived from heaven or men presume to establish it for themselves. In this lesson we will consider how important it is to begin with acceptance of a common source of authority in talking to our friends.

> To help someone learn the truth we must start with a common source of authority.

I. How Do Men Presume Authority for Themselves?

A. Men presume to establish authority for themselves when they follow the "commandments and doctrines of men" (Col. 2:18-23). Many things are done in religion that are in truth merely **"self-imposed."**

1. **Jesus rebuked the Jews for following the "tradition of the elders" to the neglect of God's word** (Matt. 15:1-6). Even though such traditions may be widespread and accepted for generations, if they are contrary to God's will as revealed in His word, they must be rejected.

2. **Some teach that the church possesses authority unto itself, separate and distinct from the authority of Scripture.** As a result, when a practice is not found in Scripture, but followed by a religious

organization, the so-called "authority of the church" is appealed to in order to justify the practice.

> **Emotions are unreliable and changing. Divine will is not revealed by strong feelings in the heart**

    a. The church that Jesus established derives all authority from Christ (Eph. 1:22-23). He is the Head over **"all things"** to His church.

    b. The word of Christ will judge men on the Day of Judgment (John 12:47-49). The church will not serve as a standard of judgment when we stand before God.

    c. Church leaders can err and practice things that are wrong (Gal. 2:11-13). The only authority that the church or its leaders possess is the responsibility to call men unto obedience to the word of God.

B. Men presume authority for themselves when they rely upon their own feelings. Many people justify various practices in religion because they come to have strong emotional feelings within themselves that God approves of their actions.

    1. Paul acted with a good conscience while persecuting the church (Acts 23:1; 1 Tim. 1:12-13). It is possible to feel that something is right when it is actually sinful.

    2. The way of man "is not in himself" (Jer. 10:23). God has not created man with an inborn instinct or moral directive that guides our behavior. The conscience can be weak (1 Cor. 8:7), seared (1 Tim. 4:2), or even evil (Heb. 10:22).

II. How Can We Make Sure That We Have Divine Authority for What We Do?

A. We must recognize the absolute authority of Scripture. God has revealed His word to mankind in the writings of the Bible. It is the absolute authority for man in this age and the means by which we can determine Divine authority for teaching and practice.

    1. Scriptures can make one "wise unto salvation" (2 Tim. 3:14-15). The Bible reveals the plan of salvation God has offered in Jesus Christ.

2. Scripture gives one all things needed **"for doctrine, for reproof, for correction, for instruction in righteousness"** (2 Tim. 3:16-17). By following the Bible one can be **"thoroughly equipped"** to be pleasing to God. Nothing else is needed.

B. We must "rightly divide" the word of truth (2 Tim. 2:15). Like any written material, one must make certain that he properly applies and interprets the Bible.

1. Some **"twist"** the Scriptures to their own destruction (2 Pet. 3:14-16). Not every teaching that claims to have Biblical authority is valid.

2. We must **"test the spirits"** (1 John 4:1). Only then can we be certain that we are following Divine authority.

C. We must recognize that the Bible can be understood (Eph. 3:1-4). Some have claimed that the Bible cannot be understood, but is a mysterious text only scholars or church leaders can unravel. While the Bible urges teachers to teach and explain the gospel (Acts 8:31), Paul shows us that we can understand the **"mystery"** when we read it. Like any written work, this involves considering...

1. *What does it instruct?* We could call these **Direct Commands** (cf. Matt. 28:19-20). Jesus teaches that we must follow His instructions. These come to us through what Jesus said while on earth and what He revealed through the Holy Spirit to His apostles (John 16:13).

2. *What does it describe?* Not all examples reflect the approval of God. Not all examples reflect the practice of His chosen apostles. **Approved Apostolic Examples**, however, teach us what we may do in order to please God (cf. Phil. 4:9). As those to whom Jesus gave the Holy Spirit, the approved examples set forth by the apostles becomes a binding standard for teaching and practice. The Holy Spirit speaks of the early prophets and apostles as a part of the **"foundation"** of the church, with Jesus as the **"Chief cornerstone"** (Eph. 2:20).

> The Bible is written communication from God to man that can be discerned just like any other text.

3. *What does it infer?* We could call these **Necessary Inferences**, or inescapable conclusion**s** (cf. Acts 20:7). When communicating information in written form a writer often makes inferences that further complete instructions and descriptions given to a reader. The text in Acts 20:7 shows by clear inference that the Christians described came together on Sunday to **"break bread"** (i.e. observe the Lord's Supper). We can thus infer necessarily that it was Divinely authorized for them to do so.

Conclusion.

he Bible allows us to have all that we need to act with the authority of heaven. Our challenge is to believe it, accept it, and faithfully obey it.

Study Questions

1. The "tradition of the elders" was a body of oral teaching that developed by the time of the first century and recorded what Jewish teachers believed about how the Law of Moses should be followed. After the New Testament, this was written down in the Jewish text known as the *Mishnah*. Explain the tradition Jesus cites in Matthew 15:1-6 that He says "made the commandment of God of no effect" in following it. _____

_____

_____

_____

_____

2. The Roman Catholic Church teaches a doctrine known as *Apostolic Succession* that claims that the authority of the apostles was passed down to leaders of the church throughout history. From this, it is argued that the Church forms a separate, but equal, standard of authority with Scripture. How does Jesus' teaching in John 12:47-49

> The teachings and examples set by Christ's apostles are a binding standard for conduct in Christ.

show that this cannot be true? _____

_____

_____

3. Many people argue that the Holy Spirit continues to directly reveal things to people today. We will explore this further in lesson seven. Some believe this *revelation* is shown by strong feelings within the heart. How does the example of Paul in Acts 23:1 refute this view?

_____

_____

_____

4. If Paul commands Timothy to "rightly divide" the word of truth what does it infer can be done (2 Tim. 2:15)? _____

_____

5. Throughout history some religious groups have taught that only religious authorities can properly understand Scripture. Others have argued that the Holy Spirit must operate on the heart to allow men to understand Scripture. How do Paul's words in Ephesians 3:1-4 address these false doctrines? _____

_____

_____

6. What did Paul tells the Philippians would result if they followed his apostolic example (Phil. 4:9)? Would not the same be true for us today? _____

_____

_____

7. Explain the sense in which Paul in Ephesians 2:20 says the apostles are part of the foundation of the church. _____

_____

_____

_____

8. List some other examples of necessary inferences in Scripture.

_____

_____

_____

Lesson Three
Original Sin

Read: Genesis 3:1-7. The account of the sin that led Adam and Eve to be cast out of the garden of Eden is the first tragedy recorded in Scripture. Much of the religious world, however, has taken the real tragedy of this event and suggested that its effect on the descendants of the first couple was much different than the Bible teaches. This misrepresentation significantly affects how one views sin, its consequences, and the remedy God offers for it.

I. What Does the Bible Say About Adam's Sin?

A. The Account in Genesis.

1. **God told the first couple not to eat of the Tree of the Knowledge of Good and Evil** (Gen. 2:16-17). The Serpent tempted Eve and she ate of the tree and gave to Adam also (Gen. 3:1-6). When this happened they received a consciousness of their own nakedness and tried to cover themselves (Gen. 3:7). The Lord confronted them and assigned punishments to them. The Serpent was consigned to crawl upon its belly (Gen. 3:8-15). The woman was given pain in childbirth (Gen. 3:16). The man was consigned to work in order to live (Gen. 3:17-19). The punishments imposed upon the man and the woman were passed down to all of their posterity as a consequence of this sin.

> Of the punishments given to Adam and Eve nothing was said about sin being passed on to their descendants.

2. Because of Adam's sin they were also cast out of the garden, depriving them of access to the Tree of Life (Gen. 3:22-24). Since all of Adam's descendants must also live outside of Eden, we are likewise deprived of access to the Tree of Life.

B. *Adam in the Epistles of Paul.* Paul in two texts makes reference to Adam and the effect of his sin.

1. **"Through one man entered the world"** (Rom. 5:12-21). In the context of demonstrating the sinfulness of mankind and our need for redemption through the gospel of Christ, Paul compares what Jesus did and its effects, with what Adam did and its effects. Paul declares plainly that **"death spread to all because all sinned"** (5:12). Adam set the example. Adam made sin possible just as Jesus made salvation possible. In Paul's illustration, Adam's sin did not automatically condemn all, any more than Jesus' righteous act automatically saved all. Both involve choice.

2. **"As in Adam all die"** (1 Cor. 15:20-26). Here, Paul is focusing on the resurrection and physical death. Adam's sin resulted in all of his descendants being subject to death because they were cut off from the Tree of Life. Jesus' resurrection resulted in the fact that one day all will be resurrected.

> Paul's comparisons between Jesus and Adam illustrate the scope of the actions of both.

II. Can Sin Be Inherited?

A. The Law of Moses (Deut. 24:16). The Law taught that fathers could not be put to death for the sins of their children nor children for the sins of their fathers. This was followed during the history of the Israelites (2 Kings 14:6; 2 Chron. 25:4).

B. The Prophet Ezekiel.

1. **During the time of the Babylonian exile, many Jews felt as if they were being held accountable for their ancestors' sins** (Ezek. 18:1-4). The Lord rebuked the Israelites for using this proverb and went on to explain that each individual bears his or her own sin.

2. **"The son shall not bear the guilt of the father"** (Ezek. 18:20). The Lord's rebuke of the Jews through Ezekiel makes it clear that the guilt of sin cannot be passed on to one's descendants.

C. The Nature of Christ.

1. **The Bible teaches that Jesus was a descendant of Adam** (Luke 3:23-38) and that He shared the fleshly nature common to mankind (Heb. 2:14-18).

Original Sin

2. The Bible also teaches that Jesus was without sin (Heb. 4:15). If Jesus was a descendant of Adam and yet was free of sin, it is clear that Adam's sin is not inherited by his posterity.

III. False Doctrines.

A. Original Sin.

1. Many in the religious world teach that all human beings are born guilty of Adam's sin and stand condemned before God because of this inheritance. As a result of this false teaching, other false teachings have been adopted, such as infant "baptism" which they claim washes away *original sin*.

2. Jesus taught that children possess the nature and character of citizens of the kingdom of heaven (Matt. 19:13-14). This could not be the case if children come into the world guilty of sin.

B. "Sinful Nature."

1. Some expanding upon the false doctrine of original sin have taught that Adam's sin has given man a "sinful nature" which can only sin unless forced to do otherwise by the Holy Spirit. The popular translation known as the *New International Version* reflected a bias towards this false doctrine in its first editions, frequently translating the word meaning simply *flesh*—"sinful nature" (see Rom. 8:1-8).

2. The Bible teaches that our fleshly nature can choose either good or evil (Ezek. 18:30-32). The flesh may be said to be weak (Matt. 26:41), but it cannot be considered inherently sinful (Acts 2:30).

Conclusion.

> If Jesus was a descendant of Adam and yet free of sin, sin is not passed down from Adam.

ankind has not inherited the sins of Adam. All souls come into this world free of sin. Each of us has the choice to do right or wrong. In spite of the fact that all accountable souls at some point do choose to sin—the example of Jesus shows that man does not have to sin nor does he possess a "sinful nature."

Study Questions

1. A common false teaching in the religious world is that as a result of Adam's sin all human beings inherit a nature *bent* towards evil. In the biblical account the only change of *nature* (if you will) that comes to the man and woman is actually said to be "like" Deity (see Gen. 3:22). Explain this account and how it refutes the idea that man's nature is inclined towards evil. _____

   _____

   _____

   _____

2. Religious teachers try to argue that Paul's declaration that because of Adam's sin "death spread to all because all sinned" (Rom. 5:12) means "all sinned *in Adam*." Two chapters earlier Paul used the exact same wording in the original language declaring "all have sinned and fallen short of the glory of God" (Rom. 3:23). Is that text describing something Adam did, or what we have done as individuals? _____

   Why would we take Romans 5:12 any differently? _____

   _____

   _____

   _____

3. Does the context of 1 Corinthians 15:20-26 indicate whether Paul is talking about spiritual death or physical death? _____

   _____

   How did Adam's sin cause physical death to come to all human beings (Gen. 3:22-24)? _____

   _____

   _____

   _____

> **Although all accountable souls choose to sin, the Bible does not teach that we have a "sinful nature."**

Original Sin

4. Explain the situations described in 2 Kings 14:6 and 2 Chronicles 25:4 and how they relate to the Mosaic teaching concerning children being put to death for the crimes of their fathers. If sin is passed down from Adam would it violate this principle? _____

_____

_____

_____

5. Fill in the blanks of the proverb God rebuked the Israelites for saying against Him in Ezekiel 18:2 "the _____ have eaten _____ _____, and the _____'s teeth are _____ on _____" (NKJV).

6. Ezekiel 18:20 makes the bold assertion that the "son shall not bear the guilt of the father." What does this tell us about the false doctrine that all of Adam's *sons* (so to speak) bear the guilt of their father Adam? _____

_____

_____

_____

7. A common argument to explain how Jesus could be a descendant of Adam and yet be free of sin is to claim that Jesus possessed Adam's supposed original uncorrupted nature. When the Hebrew writer asserts boldly that Jesus was "without sin" (Heb. 4:15), only two chapters earlier he explained that what made Jesus a suitable High Priest is the fact that He has "partaken of flesh and blood" and "shared in the same" as "the children." If His human nature was different from that of "the children" did He "share in the same"? _____

_____

_____

8. What do Jesus' words in Matthew 19:13-14 indicate regarding the unscriptural practice of infant baptism? _____

_____

9. Acts 2:30 uses the same word translated "flesh" of Jesus' nature that the original *New International Version* translated "sinful nature" in Romans 8:1-8. Did Jesus have a "sinful nature"? _____

_____

Lesson Four
Denominationalism

Human beings like making choices based upon our individual preferences. Each of us decides what foods to eat, clothes to wear, car to drive, or career to pursue based upon what we think and feel. Unfortunately, many people apply this same thinking to religious matters. They conclude that if a religious institution appeals to their own preferences then that it is "the church for them." In modern times many religious groups have grown into huge congregations as a result of surveys and market research indicating what people in the community "want in a church." In this lesson we will consider problems with this approach to religious service.

I. How Many Churches Did Jesus Build?

A. Jesus built only one church (Matt. 16:13-18). Jesus did not establish different churches teaching and practicing different things. The practices of modern times are the invention of man.

> **1. It was part of the eternal purpose of God** (Eph. 3:8-11). The church was important enough to God that He planned its institution from eternity past. Mankind should be obliged to respect God's wisdom in planning the church and not seek to alter or reshape it to our own wishes.

B. The church Jesus built is His body (Col. 1:18, 24). The church is described with the figure of Jesus' body. This figure illustrates its importance in the mind of God. Christ's body was the valuable offering that was sacrificed for the sin of the world.

> **1. There is only "one body"** (Eph. 4:1-6). Jesus did not have multiple bodies. His church, therefore is not made up of multiple bodies of doctrine and practice.

> Man must not seek to alter and reshape that which was in the mind of God from eternity past.

Denominationalism

2. **Paul taught the same thing "in every church"** (1 Cor. 4:17). The church of the New Testament was to be united in doctrine and practice.

3. **The New Testament is the guide for how the church should conduct itself** (1 Tim. 3:14-15). The standard for church conduct is not found in human creeds, councils, surveys, or opinion polls, but in the revealed will of God as set forth in the New Testament.

II. What Does the Bible Say About Religious Division?

A. **Jesus prayed that His disciples would be one** (John 17:20-23). This makes it clear that Jesus' desire and intention was for believers to be unified in doctrine and practice.

> We must not be content with a condition that runs counter to Christ's prayer for unity.

1. **Religious division was condemned** (1 Cor. 1:10-13). While there was already some religious division in the early church it was condemned and rebuked. How can we imagine it can be acceptable to God today?

2. **To be divided was considered "carnal" and not spiritual** (1 Cor. 3:3-4). While the flesh is not sinful in-and-of itself, there are sins of the flesh. As Paul uses the term **"carnal"** to describe the Corinthians he is addressing sinful works of the flesh and counts religious division among things that are **"carnal."**

B. **Following human traditions rather than the word of God was condemned** (Matt. 15:7-9). The Pharisees were never rebuked for following God's word, but they were rebuked for following human traditions to the violation or neglect of God's word.

1. **To change what had been revealed was condemned** (Gal. 1:8-9). Paul rebuked the Galatians for accepting a **"different gospel."** We must avoid the same error today.

2. **New Testament Christians were told to follow what the apostles revealed** (2 Thess. 2:13-15). The doctrine and practice of Christ's church was not to be ever-changing with each new generation. It was to be followed in accordance with the apostolic example in successive generations.

III. Whose Preferences Should Govern Religious Matters?

A. God is seeking those who will worship Him "in spirit and truth" (John 4:21-24). God wants mankind to worship Him *in truth.* These words show us that it is possible to worship in error. In so doing we would clearly be doing what God does not want.

   1. Christians should seek to be "well-pleasing" to God (2 Cor. 5:7-9). The purpose of faith is not to please ourselves but God.

   2. Even Jesus did not seek His own will, but yielded to the desires of God the Father (Luke 22:42). If God the Son was willing to forgo His own desires to do the will of God the Father shouldn't we do the same?

B. The Holy Spirit promised a time when men would follow their own desires in religion (2 Tim. 4:3-4). This shows us that God is not pleased when men simply follow their own desires as the standard in religious affairs.

   1. Christians must "turn away" from religion led by those who are "lovers of themselves" (2 Tim. 3:1-5).

> In worship to God it is His desire, not our own, that must be our concern.

Conclusion.

e live in an age in which there are almost as many different types of churches as there are human personalities. This is not how the Lord intended it to be! This is not pleasing to Him. We must look to God's word as our guide so that believers can be united in doctrine and practice.

Study Questions.

1. Many in the modern world argue that one can be in Christ but does not have to be a member of any church. How do Paul's words in Ephesians 3:8-11 address this false concept of Christ's church?

Denominationalism

_____

_____

_____

2. In Paul's epistle to the church in Colosse, after first declaring the headship of Christ over the church (1:18), he states further that God "gave Him to be head over all things to the church" (1:22). How does this address the view that religious authorities over different churches can set their own rules and laws? _____

_____

_____

3. In some people's view, the Bible is set forth as a guide for general principles but was never intended to regulate how a church operates. How do Paul's words in 1 Timothy 3:14-15 refute this false view?

_____

_____

4. In Jesus' prayer that believers be one, what effect does He indicate such unity can have on the world around us (John 17:20-23)?

_____

_____

5. Define the word "carnal" as it is used in 1 Corinthians 3:3-4. In light of its meaning in this text can we hold that religious division is pleasing to God? _____

_____

_____

6. In the first chapters of Paul's epistle to the churches of Galatia, what appear to have been some of the beliefs he identifies as accepting "another gospel" (1:8-9)? What does this indicate about modern practices and beliefs that are not taught in Scripture? _____

_____

_____

7. Based on 2 Corinthians 5:7-9 and 2 Timothy 4:3-4, whose preferences should govern what is done in religion? _____

_____

_____

Lesson Five
Baptism

Introduction.

hile most of the religious world teaches some type of baptism, there is great confusion and diversity regarding the proper method of baptism, who constitutes a suitable candidate for baptism, and the purpose and significance of baptism. In this lesson we will wade through this confusion and consider the simple New Testament teaching on the subject of baptism.

I. What is Baptism?

A. The meaning of the word.

1. The word translated **"baptize"** in the New Testament is the Greek word *baptizo* (βαπτίζω) meaning: "properly, *to dip repeatedly, to immerge, submerge*" (*Thayer's Greek-English Lexicon of the New Testament,* 94).

2. The noun, *baptisma* (βάπτισμα) translated **"baptism"** means: "*immersion, submersion*" (*ibid.*). Our English word is not really a translation but a *transliteration* of the Greek word. That is, it has been brought into English without being translated. The word means "immersion."

> The English word "baptism" is a *transliteration* not a translation. The word itself means "immersion."

B. The use of the word in the Greek Old Testament. The translation of the Old Testament, done before the time of Christ, and popular in New Testament times illustrates the use of the word.

1. Naaman is described as having "dipped" (*baptizo*) seven times in the Jordan river (2 Kings 5:14). This makes it clear that the word was used to describe a complete submersion.

Baptism

C. The use of the word in the New Testament.

1. When Philip baptized the Ethiopian eunuch both are described as going **"down into"** and coming **"up out of"** the water (Acts 8:38-39). This would only be necessary if the eunuch's baptism was a complete immersion in water.

2. **Paul likens baptism to a burial** (Rom. 6:1-6). Sprinkling and pouring do not compare in likeness to burial. There is no example in Scripture of sprinkling or pouring being substituted for or described as baptism.

II. Who Needs to Be Baptized?

A. New Testament candidates for baptism.

> All candidates for baptism in the New Testament are said to be mature and accountable for his or her choices.

1. **Simon the sorcerer was mature** (Acts 8:9, 13).

2. **The Ethiopian eunuch was mature** (Acts 8:36).

3. **Saul was mature** (Acts 9:17-18). There is no example of a newborn infant being baptized in the New Testament. All candidates for baptism are mature and accountable for their actions and choices.

B. Prerequisites for baptism.

1. **One must believe in Jesus in order to be a candidate for baptism** (Mark 16:15-16). A newborn infant is not capable of belief or disbelief so he or she is not a suitable candidate for baptism.

2. **One must repent of his or her sins in order to be a candidate for baptism** (Acts 2:36-38). A newborn infant is not guilty of sin or capable of repentance so he or she is not a suitable candidate for baptism.

III. What is The Purpose and Significance of Baptism?

A. John's Baptism. Even before Jesus began to teach baptism, John the Baptist was teaching a **"baptism of repentance for the forgiveness of sins"** (Mark 1:4).

1. **In Ephesus, Paul encountered some who had received John's baptism but not Christ's** (Acts 19:1-7). They were taught the distinction between the two and instructed to be baptized into Christ. This account teaches us that baptism must be carried out for the proper purpose in order for it to be acceptable to the Lord.

B. Baptism and salvation.

1. **Baptism is necessary for salvation** (1 Pet. 3:18-22). It is **"an appeal to God for a good conscience"** (NASB).

2. **In baptism one may "put on" Christ** (Gal. 3:26-27). The Bible does not describe someone as having "put on Christ" or being "in Christ" prior to or without baptism.

3. **In baptism one can "wash away" his or her sins** (Acts 22:14-16). Paul was not forgiven of his sins prior to his baptism, but needed to be baptized in order to receive forgiveness of sins.

> Baptism into Christ must be done for the proper purpose and significance.

Conclusion.

It is clear from Scripture that baptism is an act of immersion or submersion in water. It is carried out on those who are mature, accountable, and who have first come to believe in Jesus and have repented of their sins. Baptism is necessary for salvation and the means by which one "puts on" Christ and washes away his or her sins through the blood of Christ.

Baptism

1. Explain the difference between a *transliteration* and a *translation*. What would a proper translation be of the word *baptisma*? _____
   _____
   _____

2. The Old Testament was written in Hebrew, but a translation of it into Greek was done before the time of the New Testament. What does the example of Naaman in 2 Kings 5:14 as recorded in the Greek Old Testament illustrate about words translated "baptize" or "baptism" in 2 Kings 5:14? _____
   _____
   _____

3. One false doctrine often leads to other false doctrines. What did we note in lesson three that led people to believe that infant baptism was necessary in the first place? What were the Scriptural problems with this view? _____
   _____
   _____
   _____
   _____

4. List two prerequisites to baptism listed in Mark 16:15-16 and Acts 2:38. 1) _____ and 2) _____
   Can an infant do these things? _____
   _____

5. Many argue that one can be saved before he or she is baptized. How does 1 Peter 3:21 refute this view? _____
   _____

6. Paul taught the Galatians that in baptism one may "put on" Christ (Gal. 3:26-27). Is one *in Christ* if he has not *put on* Christ? _____
   _____

7. Many teach Paul was saved on the road to Damascus. If he still needed to "wash away" sins (Acts 22:16) can this be true? _____

Lesson Six
Instrumental Music

Introduction.

One of the most common questions that is posed to Christians concerns what the Bible teaches about musical worship to God. To consider this, let's start by considering some basic principles regarding God's attitude toward worship offered to Him.

I. "Unless the Lord builds the house..." (Psa. 127:1).

This text suggests to us that it is important that man only put his trust in that which God has established. In all ages God has revealed what He wants man to do in to worship Him. In all ages to act on one's own imagination in matters of worship is condemned.

A. **Cain and Abel** (Gen. 4:3-5; Heb. 11:4). The Hebrew writer tells us that Abel acted by faith. True faith is based upon the instruction of God (Rom. 10:17). Abel obeyed God's instruction but Cain did not.

B. **David and the Ark of the Covenant** (1 Chron. 13:6-14; 15:2, 12-15). When David sought to return the ark to Jerusalem he first set it on a cart. Uzzah died in connection with this. David came to realize that God had instructed that only Levites were to carry the ark on poles.

C. **Jeroboam's Feast Days** (1 Kings 12:32, 33; 14:7-10). Jeroboam established his own religious festivals, rejecting the Law of Moses and was condemned for his apostasy.

D. **Uzziah's Incense** (2 Chron. 26:16-20). King Uzziah presumed to take upon himself the right to burn incense in the temple, a duty exclusively given to priests. When he did so the Lord struck him with leprosy.

> The Bible gives examples of things done as acts of worship that were not acceptable to God.

27

Instrumental Music

1. These examples show us that God expects His word to be followed and neither altered or amended.

II. Different Covenants — Different Standards.

Just as God has revealed His expectations to man at different times throughout human history it is clear that God has set different standards at different times, under different covenants.

A. **Moses and the Rock** (Exod. 17:5-6; Num. 20:7-12). On two occasions God brought forth water from rock, Moses was given different instructions each time. When Moses the second time did what he was told to do the first time he was prohibited from entering Canaan.

B. **Priests Before and After Moses.** All throughout human history there have been men identified as priests of God.

1. **Patriarchal Age** (Gen. 14:18). Melchizedek was a priest long before Levi or Aaron were even born.

2. **The Law of Moses** (Exod. 28:1). Under the Law of Moses only those of the tribe of Levi, who were descended from Aaron could serve as priests.

3. **The Law of Christ** (Rev. 1:6; 5:10). Under Christ, all Christians are priests regardless of tribe.

> The same action allowed under one covenant may be unlawful under a second.

C. **Jeroboam's Priests** (2 Chron. 13:9-11). When Jeroboam rejected the Law of Moses and appointed priests from all tribes it was condemned, in spite of the fact that later under Christ all believers would become priests.

1. These examples show that the same things may occur at different times, and yet be either acceptable or condemned based upon what God has authorized under the particular covenant.

III. Under the Law of Moses, God Instructed the Use of Mechanical Instruments of Music.

A. Dedication of the Temple (2 Chron. 5:11-14). A variety of instruments were used upon the dedication of the temple, as the ark was put in place, and the glory of the Lord filled the temple.

B. The Psalms (Psa. 55:1; 150:4). The Psalms in both their introductory instructions and in their content command instrumental music. Jesus said the Psalms were inspired by the Holy Spirit (Mark 12:36; Psa. 110:1).

C. Hezekiah's Passover (2 Chron. 29:25). As this text describes Hezekiah's observation of the Passover, it reveals that the use of instrumental music in Mosaic temple worship was commanded by God through the prophets.

> In the Old Testament the use of mechanical instruments of music was commanded.

1. Although approved during the Mosaic age, God did express displeasure with how some carried out this type of worship (Amos 5:23; 6:3-5).

IV. Under the Law of Christ Only Singing is Instructed.

A. Examples of disciples singing.

1. Jesus and the disciples at the institution of the Lord's Supper (Matt. 26:30; Mark 14:26).

2. Paul and Silas in prison (Acts 16:25).

B. Instructions about singing.

1. Christians are to speak to one another by singing (Eph. 5:19).

2. Christians are to teach one another by singing (Col. 3:16).

3. Christians are to sing when happy (James 5:13).

4. Singing is to be done **"with the understanding"** of what is being sung (1 Cor. 14:15).

Instrumental Music

5. Old Testament Scriptures referring to singing are applied to Christians (Rom. 15:8-9; Heb. 2:11-12).

6. Given that mechanical instruments in worship played such an important role in Old Testament worship, the total lack of any instruction to use them in the New Testament is conspicuous, compelling, and very significant.

C. There is no example or instruction in the New Testament of Christians worshipping God with mechanical instruments of music under the Law of Christ.

1. The only New Testament references to mechanical instruments of music in worship refer to conditions in heaven, not the worship of Christians on earth in this age (Rev. 15:2-3).

Conclusion.

There is no authority under the Law of Christ to worship God with mechanical instruments of music. To do so would be to act presumptuously and without authority. Such action is always condemned. Christians are commanded to sing in worship to God. We must do so fervently, diligently, and from the heart.

Study Questions

1. It is often assumed that if something is done as an act of worship, so long as it is not inherently wicked it must be acceptable to God. List the acts of worship and respect to God done by the following people:
   a) Cain (Gen. 4:3-5) _____
   b) David (1 Chron. 13:6-14; 15:2-15) _____
   _____
   c) Jeroboam (1 Kings 12:32, 33; 14:7-10) _____
   _____
   d) Uzziah (2 Chron. 26:16-20) _____
   Were these things inherently wicked? _____

2. What determines whether something is sinful is not whether it seems inherently wicked, but whether God has commanded or forbidden it. What act did Moses do that was acceptable at one time yet forbidden on a separate occasion (see Exod. 17:5-6; Num. 20:7-12)?

_____

What resulted when Moses did this? _____

_____

_____

3. Under the Law of Moses what ancestry requirements did one have to meet to be a priest (Exod. 28:1)? How was this changed under Christ (Rev. 1:6; 5:10)? _____

_____

4. In the past some brethren argued that the Jews in the Old Testament presumed for themselves to use mechanical instruments of music in worship. What does 2 Chronicles 29:25 indicate to us that shows that God had commanded it? _____

_____

5. The fact that God commanded the use of mechanical instruments of music in worship in the Old Testament does not mean that it is approved in the New Testament. List the four instructions given in the New Testament regarding musical worship to God. a) Ephesians 5:19: _____

_____

b) Colossians 3:16: _____

_____

c) James 5:13:_____

_____

d) 1 Corinthians 4:15: _____

_____

6. Are there any New Testament commands to use mechanical instruments? _____

7. What is the context of the only reference to instruments in worship in the New Testament (Rev. 15:2-3)? _____
Does this set a precedent for us? _____

Lesson Seven
The Holy Spirit

Introduction.

Before Jesus ascended into heaven He promised the apostles that the Holy Spirit, whom He described as the "Helper," would come upon them in power (Acts 1:8). This promise was fulfilled shortly after His ascension when the Holy Spirit fell upon the apostles on the day of Pentecost. On that day they spoke in tongues and began to act under the guidance and direction of the Holy Spirit. There is much confusion in the religious world regarding the purpose, duration, and effect of this event on Christians today. In this lesson we will consider this event and its consequences.

I. To Whom was the Holy Spirit Promised?

A. Jesus promises to His apostles (Matt. 10:5a, 19-20; John 14:25-26; 16:12-14). Jesus told His apostles that the Holy Spirit would give them power, knowledge, and the ability to answer when they were questioned.

> The promises to the apostles were unique and were not made to all Christians.

B. The authority of the apostles (Eph. 2:19-22; 1 Cor. 14:37). The apostles were given authority to teach the commandments of the Lord. This authority allowed them to be considered part of the foundation of the church.

C. The laying on of hands.

1. Simon the sorcerer (Acts 8:14-20). This event shows that the apostles possessed special authority to pass on the Holy Spirit in power through the laying on of hands. There is no indication that this authority passed on to anyone else.

2. **Paul's instructions to Timothy** (1 Tim. 4:13-14; 2 Tim. 2:15). Even though Timothy had been given some type of spiritual gift, unlike the apostles who did not have to study ahead of time what they should say, Paul told Timothy to study and read to prepare himself. This shows that the effect of the Holy Spirit on believers other than the apostles, did not impart to them internal direction without study.

II. Were Miraculous Spiritual Gifts to Endure?

A. What was the purpose of miraculous spiritual gifts?

1. **Miracles confirmed the word** (Mark 16:17-20).

2. **God bore witness to the gospel through miracles** (Heb. 2:1-4).

3. **Miracles were not always applied to common problems of life.**

   a. **Epaphroditus nearly died** (Phil. 2:25-28).

   b. **Paul's thorn in the flesh was not removed** (2 Cor. 12:7-9). Miraculous spiritual gifts were never intended to take away all illness or infirmity but were a Divine witness to the reliability and Divinity of the gospel.

> Old Testament prophecy promised the outpouring of miraculous gifts and their end.

B. Old Testament promises regarding miraculous spiritual gifts.

1. **The prophecy of Joel** (Joel 2:28-32).

2. **The prophecy of Zechariah** (Zech. 13:1-5). While the prophecy of Joel promised the coming of miraculous spiritual gifts during the age when the Christ reigned over His kingdom, the prophecy of Zechariah promised the end of such gifts during the same period.

C. "That which is perfect."

1. **The Corinthians' abuse of spiritual gifts** (1 Cor. 12-14). Throughout this text Paul explains to the Corinthians the proper use and purpose of spiritual gifts. It is in the context of these instructions that Paul addressed the duration of such gifts.

2. **"That which is in part will pass away"** (1 Cor. 13:8-10). In the context of 1 Corinthians, **"that which is in part"** refers to miraculous spiritual gifts. It follows then, that the **"perfect thing"** to which this text refers is not Jesus or heaven, but complete and full revelation.

III. How Does the Holy Spirit Affect Believers Today?

A. The Holy Spirit is the source of Scripture (2 Pet. 1:19-21). As a result, whenever Scripture *speaks* it may be said that the Spirit speaks (see Matt. 22:43).

B. Scripture is the "sword of the Spirit" (Eph. 6:17; Heb. 4:12-13; 1 Thess. 2:13). It is clear that the Holy Spirit works in believers through the word. There is no indication that the type of direct revelation and direction that was given to the apostles was ever intended for all believers.

> When a Christian sets his or her mind on the things the Spirit has revealed it is living "according to the Spirit."

C. Deity dwells in us "through faith."

1. The Spirit dwelling in us is the same as Christ dwelling in us (Rom. 8:10-11).

2. Christ dwells in us through faith (Eph. 3:14-17).

3. Living according to the Spirit is defined as *setting the mind* on the things of the Spirit (Rom. 8:5-8).

Conclusion.

The Bible makes it clear that the apostles were promised things that were not general promises to all believers. Some of these promises involved the special work they carried out in the establishment of the church and the confirmation of the word they taught. The Bible represents the full and final revelation of the Holy Spirit and is the means by which the Holy Spirit dwells in and works in believers today.

The Holy Spirit

1. List some of the specific promises regarding the Holy Spirit made to the apostles in the following passages.

   Matthew 10:5a, 19-20: _____

   _____

   John 14:25-26: _____

   _____

   John 16:12-14:_____

   _____

   Are there any elements of these promises that show they could only apply to the apostles? If so, what? _____

   _____

2. Explain what Acts 8:14-20 teaches regarding the laying on of the apostles' hands as it relates to the Holy Spirit._____

   _____

   _____

   _____

   Did all Christians receive the laying on of the apostles' hands?

   _____

3. How do Paul's instructions to Timothy differ from the promise Jesus gave to the apostles (cf. Matt. 10:5a, 19-20; 1 Tim. 4:13-14; 2 Tim. 2:15)? _____

   _____

   _____

   _____

4. What were some of the miraculous signs Jesus promised in Mark 16:17-18? What were these things said to confirm (Mark 16:19-20)?_____

   _____

   _____

5. Whom does Hebrews 2:1-4 say bore witness to the word spoken by the "signs and wonders" performed? _____

> Scripture is the revelation of the Holy Spirit and the means by which He dwells in believers.

The Holy Spirit

6. What does the prophecy of Joel 2:28-32 promise? _____
   When does Peter say this was fulfilled (see Acts 2:16-22)? _____
   _____
   _____

7. What does Zechariah 13:1 promise will be opened "for sin and un-
   clearness"? _____
   When was forgiveness of sins "opened" for "the house of David" and
   the inhabitants of Jerusalem? _____
   _____

8. During the time promised in Zechariah 13:1 what will "depart from
   the land" (Zech. 13:2)?_____
   _____

9. In light of the prophecies of Joel 2:28-32 and Zechariah 13:1-5,
   were miraculous gifts of the Holy Spirit intended to continue in-
   definitely during the age of Christ's reign? _____
   _____

10. What is the focus of 1 Corinthians 12-14? _____
    _____

11. What does 1 Corinthians 13:9 say was "in part" for the Corin-
    thians? _____

12. The word translated "perfect" is the Greek word *teleios* (τέλειος)
    meaning "*brought to its end, finished*" (Thayer). In light of what
    verse nine and the context identify as partial, what logically would
    be "that which is perfect" or *brought to its end*? _____
    _____

13. List the two persons of the Godhead said to dwell in a Christian in
    Romans 8:10-11. a) _____
    b) _____

14. In Ephesians 3:14-17 how does Paul say Christ dwells in a Christian?
    _____

15. How does Paul explain to the Romans that Christians may live "ac-
    cording to the Spirit" (Rom. 8:5-8)?_____
    _____

Lesson Eight
The Lord's Supper

Introduction.

On the night of Jesus' betrayal, He instituted a memorial that He commanded to be observed by His followers. In today's world confusion exists regarding the manner, frequency, and significance of this observation. In this lesson we will consider what the Bible teaches about this memorial in order to clarify these areas of confusion.

I. How Should the Lord's Supper Be Observed?

A. Who should observe the Lord's Supper? (Matt. 26:26-27; Acts 20:7). Not only did all of the disciples partake of the elements of the Lord's Supper, but after Jesus' death, all disciples observed the memorial. No element was reserved for or excluded from any Christian.

B. What elements constitute the Lord's Supper? (Luke 22:8; Exod. 12:19). The Lord's Supper was instituted while Jesus and His disciples observed the Passover. Neither bread nor grapejuice that was leavened (or fermented) could be in the house during Passover. This makes it clear that the bread and fruit of the vine that He gave to the disciples would have been unleavened bread and grape juice.

> The institution of the Lord's Supper during Passover indicates the nature of the elements.

C. Must the fruit of the vine be taken from one cup? (Luke 22:15-20). Some teach that the fruit of the vine must be shared from one cup. The account in Luke makes it clear that Jesus divided the contents of the cup among the disciples before they ate the Passover meal. This divided cup is what He later referred to as drinking of in the Kingdom and what He identified with His blood.

The Lord's Supper

II. When Should the Lord's Supper Be Observed?

A. The example of Paul in Troas (Acts 20:7). Although Jesus did not specify when the memorial was to be observed, the example of Paul in the city of Troas indicates that Christians in the New Testament did so on Sunday, the first day of the week.

B. The witness of church history. While uninspired history is obviously limited and subject to human frailty, in some cases we can see what was taught in the New Testament reflected in early practice.

> The Lord's Supper was observed by early Christians each Sunday, the first of the week.

1. **Justin Martyr** (ca. 150 AD). After describing the observance of the Lord's Supper, he claimed, "We hold this common gathering on Sunday, since it is the first day, on which God, transforming darkness and matter, made the universe, and Jesus Christ our Savior rose from the dead on the same day" (*First Apology,* 67, Richardson).

2. *The Didache* (ca. 150 AD). In a description of worship, it claimed, "And on the Lord's own day gather yourselves together and break bread and give thanks, first confessing your transgressions that your sacrifice may be pure" (14, Lightfoot).

III. What Is the Significance of the Lord's Supper?

A. "Do this in remembrance of Me" (Luke 22:19; 1 Cor. 11:24-25). In Jesus' very instructions to the Twelve, He identified the significance of the Supper as a memorial. It is to be done remembering the death of Jesus.

B. Do the bread and fruit of the vine become the literal flesh and blood of Christ? (Eph. 2:19-22; 1 Cor. 14:37).

Some in the religious world teach that the elements of the memorial actually transform into the literal body and blood of Jesus.

1. **If so, then Jesus drank His own blood** (Matt. 26:27-29; Mark 14:24-25). When a Christian observes the Lord's Supper he is partaking of the elements with the Lord in His kingdom. Jesus did not drink His own blood on the night of His death, nor does He in the observance of the memorial.

2. **The eating of blood has always been condemned in Scripture** (Lev. 17:11-12; Acts 15:29). If a Christian eats the literal blood of Jesus in the memorial, he is violating ordinances taught in both Old and New Testaments.

> Jesus did not eat His own flesh or drink His own blood —the elements represent His body and blood.

Conclusion.

The Bible teaches that disciples of Christ observed the Lord's Supper on the first day of the week, partaking of unleavened bread and fruit of the vine in memory of Jesus' death. This was a memorial observed by the church to regularly remind them of Jesus' sacrifice for mankind. Although it does not involve any mysterious or miraculous transformation of the elements, it is a beautiful and important aspect of worship to God under the Law of Christ.

Study Questions.

1. The Roman Catholic Church used to teach that only the priest could partake of the cup when observing the Lord's Supper. Whom does Matthew 26:26-27 indicate ate of the elements? _____

   _____

   Who ate of the elements at Troas in Acts 20:7? _____

   _____

2. According to Exodus 12:19 what was to be removed from the house prior to the observation of Passover among the Jews? _____

   _____

3. Most modern Jews do not teach that fermented grape juice is con-

The Lord's Supper

sidered "leavened," however a sect known as the Kairites argues that it would have been. Exodus 12:19 one of the Hebrew words for "leaven" was *chametz*. Numbers 6:3 used *chametz* of drinks that had undergone secondary fermentation to become "vinegar." *Young's Literal Translation* translates Exodus 12:19b, "…anyone eating anything fermented—that person hath been cut off from the company of Israel…" Is there any question that grape juice is *unleavened*? _____

_____

4. When did the church in Troas observe the Lord's Supper (Acts 20:7)? Is this pattern recorded in early church history? _____

_____

5. According to 1 Corinthians 11:17-20 what is to be the context, or with what group of people is the Lord's Supper to be observed?

_____

6. One of the reasons the Roman Catholic Church deprived all members from drinking the cup is because they believe that it becomes the literal blood of Christ. Once again, one false doctrine can lead to another. In Luke 22:19 and 1 Corinthians 11:24-25 why did Jesus say His disciples were to "do this"?_____

_____

7. If the elements become Jesus' literal flesh and blood, what would that indicate that He ate with the disciples? _____

_____

8. What did Leviticus 17:11-12 forbid Jews to eat under the Law of Moses?

_____

9. What does Acts 15:29 forbid Christians to eat under the Law of Christ?

_____

10. If the elements of the Lord's Supper become the literal flesh and blood of Jesus would this violate the teaching of Acts 15:29? _____

_____

_____

_____

Lesson Nine
Eternal Security

Introduction.

The Bible teaches that those who are in Christ are saved by the blood of Jesus. The saved have the hope and promise of eternal life with God in the age to come. Many in the religious world, however, teach that this security is in no way conditioned upon a person's continued faithfulness to the Lord. In this lesson we will consider what the Bible teaches about the doctrine of "once saved, always saved" or eternal security.

I. The New Testament Warns Against Falling Away.

A. The Hebrew writer warns that those who have **"once been enlightened"** and have **"become partakers of the Holy Spirit"** and the **"powers of the age to come"** can fall away so as to **"crucify"** Jesus again (Heb. 6:4-8).

B. The Hebrew writer also warns Christians who would **"sin willfully"** that to do so is to **"trample"** Jesus under foot (Heb. 10:26-31). The writer speaks of this as a condition in which there remains **"no sacrifice"** left for sins. Without the blood of Jesus one is lost. Such are warned that it is a **"fearful thing"** to fall into the hands of the Living God.

> Without the sacrifice of Jesus no one is saved. If "no sacrifice" remains for an unfaithful Christian he is lost.

   1. If a Christian cannot sin so as to be lost why would this be a fearful thing?

C. Peter warns those who have **"escaped the pollutions of the world"** (i.e. sin), that if they become **"entangled"** in sin again the **"latter end is worse for them than the beginning"** (2 Pet. 2:18-22). Sin led to condemnation in the "**beginning.**" Would not a fate worse than the "**beginning**" mean that it is a fate worse than condemnation while in ignorance?

II. Scripture Offers Examples of Those Who Fell Away.

A. Ananias and Sapphira were a husband and wife in the church in Jerusalem who conspired to lie to God and the apostles (Acts 5:1-11). Although they were members of the church (cf. Acts 2:47), they were struck dead for their sin.

> We can't say that Simon was never saved to begin with if Scripture tells us he "believed" and was "baptized."

B. Simon, a new convert in Samaria who had been a sorcerer tried to buy the gift of the laying on of hands, in order pass on the Holy Spirit (Acts 8:9-25).

1. Simon "**believed,**" he "**was baptized,**" and continued with Philip (Acts 8:13). The Holy Spirit thus acknowledged that He was saved.

2. Yet, Peter warned him after this sin that he could "**perish**" (Acts 8:20), that he had "**no part or portion**" with the things of God (Acts 8:21), and that he must repent and pray so that he "**may be forgiven**" and freed from sin (Acts 8:22-23). This clearly shows us that a Christian can be saved and yet sin in such a way that he or she can once again be separated from God.

C. Paul warned the Corinthians, using several examples from Israelite history that those who think they stand can fall (1 Cor. 10:1-12). This warning makes it clear that a Christian who "**stands**" can "**fall.**"

III. Security in Christ Is Conditioned Upon Faithfulness.

A. Those who are "in Christ" will be saved (Rom. 8:1). Paul shows that the condition under which one can face "**no condemnation**" is that of being "**in Christ.**"

1. We observed above that one who returns to sin "**crucifies**" Christ again and "**tramples**" Him underfoot. Such a soul cannot be considered to be "**in Christ**" (cf. Heb. 6 and 10).

B. One must **"be faithful until death"** to receive **"the crown of life"** (Rev. 2:10).

C. **The power of the word "if."** The word **"if"** in English is a conditional conjunction, meaning "a. *in the event that,* b. *granting that,* c. *on condition that*" (*American Heritage Dictionary*). The Greek word *ei* (εἰ) carries essentially the same force. When **"if"** is used in Scripture it communicates that something will occur on the condition that something else takes place.

   1. **We will be saved "if" we "hold fast" to the gospel** (1 Cor. 15:1-2). This demands that we understand Paul to warn that **"if"** we do not **"hold fast"** we will be lost.

   2. **We are disciples "if" we abide in Christ** (John 15:1-8). This demands that we understand Jesus to warn that **"if"** we do not abide in His words we are not His disciples.

   3. **"If" we "walk in the light" and confess our sins to God we can be forgiven** (1 John 1:5-2:2). This demands that we understand John (through the Holy Spirit) to teach that **"if"** we do not **"walk in the light"** and **"confess our trespasses"** we will not have forgiveness and Christ's blood will not cleanse our sins.

> We must help our friends understand that sin places one's soul in jeopardy.

Conclusion.

The Bible makes it clear that a person can obey the gospel and then sin in such a way as to be lost and separated from God once again. There is security that rests in Christ, but this security is conditioned upon abiding in Christ and in His word. To teach otherwise is to diminish the necessity of Christ's death and mock the very justice of God.

Study Questions.

1. A common argument by advocates of "once saved always saved" is that if someone falls away after coming to Christ the person

was "never really saved to begin with!" List five conditions described in Hebrews 6:4-5 that applied to one before falling away that refute this false claim. a) _____

b) _____

c) _____

d) _____

e) _____

2. Can one be saved if "no sacrifice" remains for his or her sin (cf. Heb. 10:26-31)? _____

_____

3. In 2 Peter 2:22 he uses two illustrations to show what it is like for one who returns to sin after coming to Christ? List these illustrations.

a) _____

b) _____

Do either of these illustrations teach "once saved always saved"?

_____

4. List three things in the account of Simon the sorcerer in Acts 8:9-25 that make it clear that he was not secure in the sin he had committed, but had to turn from it in order to once again be right with God. a) _____

b) _____

c) _____

5. In Romans 8:1 the majority of surviving manuscripts include the phrase at the end of the verse "who do not walk according to the flesh, but according to the Spirit." This is reflected in the *King James* and *New King James* Translations. Because the phrase in missing in a few of the oldest surviving manuscripts translations such as the *American Standard, New American Standard,* and *English Standard Version* omit these words. All manuscripts restate these words at the end of Romans 8:4. In all translations of Romans 8:1, under what condition does Paul teach that one may have "no condemnation"? _____

_____

6. Under what condition does Paul tell the Corinthians they will be saved (1 Cor. 15:1-2)? _____

Lesson Ten
Women's Role in the Church

Introduction.

The Bible assigns specific roles to men and women in the home and in the church. These roles limit the responsibilities and behavior of both men and women. In our generation, many in the religious world have rejected these Biblically assigned roles and presumed to give to men and women the same roles in both the home and the church. In this lesson we will consider what the Bible teaches about a woman's role in the local church.

I. Scriptural Instructions Regarding Women.

A. "Let your women keep silent in the churches" (1 Cor. 14:34-35).

1. The word **"silent"** here is the Greek word *sigao* (σιγάω) meaning—"To keep silence, hold one's peace; passively to be kept in silence, be concealed" (*Thayer's Greek English Lexicon of the New Testament,* 574). Further, "1. Be silent, keep still. a. say nothing keep silent. b. stop speaking, become silent…" (*A Greek English Lexicon of the New Testament and Other Early Christian Literature,* by Walter Bauer, 749).

2. **This is a word for absolute silence.** Exceptions to this would be singing (Eph. 5:19; Col. 3:16) and confession of Christ (Matt. 10:32-33). In general silence is commanded.

> Paul's instructions to the Corinthians describe restrictions when the church is assembled.

3. *In what sense is the word "church" used here?*

   a. Not the universal sense (a woman would have to be silent from the moment she became a Christian).

   b. Nor purely in the local sense (all Christians should be identified with a local congregation—she would have to be silent from the moment she identified with a local church).

c. This is when a congregation comes together as a church to engage in authorized works of the church. At that time a woman must remain silent.

B. "Let a woman learn in silence with all submission" (1 Tim. 2:8-14). Two points to note here:

1. **"Learn in SILENCE"** (NASB **"quietness"**). **"Silence"** here is translated from the Greek word *hesuchia* (ἡσυχία) meaning – "1. Quietness. 2. Silence" (*Thayer's Greek English Lexicon of the New Testament*, 281) "1. Quietness, rest. "Silence… quiet down" (*A Greek English Lexicon of the New Testament and Other Early Christian Literature,* by Walter Bauer, 349). This is not absolute silence but a disposition of quietness. The text indicates that a woman is to maintain a disposition of quietness at all times.

2. Women are not to teach or have authority over men (presumably in a religious context). Secular authority is not condemned.

C. 1 Corinthians 14:34-35 and 1 Timothy 2:11-12 compared. We note that these texts address different contexts and offer different instructions and prohibitions.

1. *1 Corinthians 14:34-35.*

   a. **Context:** Spiritual gifts and conduct in the church assembly.

   b. **Instruction:** **"Keep silent."**

   c. **Prohibition:** Not permitted to speak.

2. *1 Timothy 2:11-12.*

   a. **Context:** General conduct.

   b. **Instruction:** Learn in **"quietness"** (ASV) or **"quietly"** (NASB).

   c. **Prohibition:** Not permitted to teach or have authority over a man.

D. "Teachers of good things" (Titus 2:1-5).

> Paul's words to Timothy address general conduct in or out of the church assembly.

1. Some contend that 1 Timothy prohibits a woman from teaching in any context. However, this passage commands women to be **"teachers of good things"** (v. 3) and older women to **"admonish the younger women...."**

2. This makes it clear that outside of the assembly a woman may teach other women and children.

3. *Is there any context in which a woman may speak with a man about spiritual matters?* We have already seen that a wife may talk with her husband at home about spiritual things (1 Cor. 14:35). In addition to this...

> Outside of a church assembly Priscilla, with her husband, explained the truth to Apollos.

E. **"They took him aside and explained to him the way of God more accurately"** (Acts 18:24-26).

1. This was not in the assembly, nor is it a woman over a man but with another man explaining the way of God. In Greek **"they"** indicates it wasn't "THEY took him aside and HE explained" but rather, **"THEY took him aside and THEY explained"**).

2. This shows that in a setting outside of the church assembly, where a woman is not over a man she may talk with men (other than her husband) about spiritual matters maintaining a quiet disposition.

II. Applications.

A. **In the church assembly a woman should not preach.**

1. This would be teaching and exercising authority over a man (1 Tim. 2:12).

2. This would be speaking in the church (1 Cor. 14:34).

B. **In the assembly a woman should not lead singing, prayer, preside at the Lord's table, or read Scripture.**

1. This would be speaking in the church (1 Cor. 14:34).

C. **In a Bible class that is not the church assembled a woman may speak but not teach over a man.**

1. A smaller portion of a congregation meeting in a home, part of a meeting house, or anywhere else does not constitute the church assembled (Acts 18:26).

2. This follows the example of Priscilla and Aquilla in Acts 18:24-26.

D. A woman may teach other women or children in settings outside of the assembly.

1. This is not speaking in the church (1 Cor. 14:34).

2. It is not exercising authority over a man (1 Tim. 2:13).

3. This follows the instructions of Titus 2:1-5.

E. In instances in which the church is assembled to carry out authorized works of the church a woman must not speak whether it is a period of worship or not.

1. Members of a local congregation are always a part of the church but they are not always **"in the church."** For example: if every member of a local church engaged in a common business it wouldn't mean that the church was engaged in that business.

2. Worship is not the only authorized work of the church (cf. Matt. 18:15-20). This would not be worship but it would involve an assembly of the church.

> **Outside of the church assembly a woman can teach women and children.**

Conclusion.

We must follow the pattern of the Bible in all things, no matter how much our culture and the religious world rejects them. God has set roles for men and women in accordance with His wisdom. We must accept this and never presume to act on our own wishes and imagination.

Women's Role in the Church

Study Questions.

1. Define the Greek word *sigao* used in 1 Corinthians 14:34. _____
   _____
   _____

2. This word is also used in 1 Corinthians 14:25, 28. Explain its use
   in those two passages. _____
   _____
   _____

   Are there any differences between what is commanded in 14:25,
   28 and the instructions to women in 14:34-35? _____
   _____
   _____

3. What do the following passages teach all Christians?
   Ephesians 5:19 and Colossians 3:16: _____
   Matthew 10:32: _____
   How can we know that these are exceptions to the restriction
   of 1 Corinthians 14:34-35? _____
   _____
   _____
   _____

4. Identify the passages below with the sense of the word "church"
   used in each text:
   a. Matthew 18:17   _____Universal sense
   b. 1 Corinthians 11:18   _____Local sense
   c. Hebrews 12:23   _____Local church assembled
   d. Matthew 16:18
   e. Revelation 2:1
   f. 2 Corinthians 1:1
   In which sense is the word used in 1 Corinthians 14:34-35?
   _____

5. Does anything in the context before or after 1 Timothy 2:8-14
   indicate to us whether Paul is talking about conduct in the assem-

bly or general conduct? If so what and where is it located? _____
_____

6. Define the word *hesuchia* used in 1 Timothy 2:11-12. How does this word differ from the word in 1 Corinthians 14:34-35? _____
_____
_____

7. Some brethren who object to the church having Bible classes for all ages have argued that 1 Timothy 2:11-12 restricts women from teaching in any formal class situation. Does Titus 2:1-5 indicate anything about the formality of the setting during which she is to be a "teacher of good things" or simply whom she is to teach? _____
_____
_____

> We must follow God's word no matter how much our world rejects its teachings.

8. How do we know that Priscilla also spoke to Apollos in Acts 18:24-26? _____
_____
_____

9. What would be wrong with having a woman preach at a church assembly (1 Cor. 14:34-35)? _____
_____

10. What would be wrong with having a woman lead prayer, singing, or preside at the Lord's table during a church assembly (1 Cor. 14:34-35; 1 Tim. 2:12)? _____
_____

11. In classes that do not involve the church assembled can a woman make comments (Acts 18:24-26)? _____
_____

12. In light of the teaching of Matthew 18:17, is a congregation assembled "as a church" when announcements are being made? Should a woman speak at this time? _____
_____
_____
_____

Lesson Eleven
The Eldership of the Church

![Introduction.]

The Bible mandates appointed leaders over local churches called (among other names) "elders." These leaders are to be chosen based upon specific qualifications and are to lead within the limits of the role outlined for them in Scripture. The religious world has seen many departures, alterations, and man-made innovations to this role which are not taught in Scripture.

I. Biblical Teachings on the Eldership.

A. Names given to the work.

1. *Presbuteros* (πρεσβύτερος) meaning **"older."** Presbyter = Elder. A form of this word is used in 1 Timothy 4:14 used of the body of elders (i.e. "the presbytry" = eldership). This name describes the role of the elders in relation to their age. They are not young and inexperienced, but they are those older in the faith.

2. *Episcopos* (ἐπίσκοπος) - meaning **"overseer."** Bishop = Overseer. This is used in Acts 20:28 and 1 Timothy 3:1. This name refers to the same role as that of elders (see Acts 20:17), but it describes the nature of their work—they *oversee* the church.

3. *Poimen* (ποιμήν) meaning **"shepherd."** Pastor = Shepherd. This is used in Acts 20:28, 1 Peter 5:1-2, and Ephesians 4:11 of the same role as that of a bishop or elder. This name also describes the nature of their work. As spiritual shepherds they are involved in feeding and protecting the flock.

> Three words are used to describe this work. Each is translated two ways in English.

B. Qualifications for service (Acts 14:23; 20:28).

1. **Paul's instructions to Timothy** (1 Tim. 3:1-7).

2. **Paul's instructions to Titus** (Titus 1:5-9).

C. Responsibilities of the eldership.

1. **Peter's teachings** (1 Pet. 5:1-5).

2. **The Hebrew writer's teachings** (Heb. 13:17).

II. Departures From the Biblical Pattern for the Authority of Eldership.

A. The expansion of authority.

> **The Bible teaches that the eldership has limited authority within the bounds of God's word.**

1. **Absolute submission.** Some churches have taught that a bishop has authority to command whether God's word has taught something or not. The "pope," the Roman Catholic bishop of Rome is said to have "papal infallibility." His commands are considered unquestionable. In many controversies, some take essentially the same view when they argue that the members of a congregation must follow the elders in matters without Scriptural authority. The Bible gives the eldership limited authority within the bounds of God's word (Acts 5:29).

2. **Expanded oversight.** Some churches have presumed to give a bishop authority over more than one church. Others, who reject this, allow practices in foreign evangelism in which elders in one country control the affairs of churches in other countries. The Bible teaches that the authority of the eldership is limited to the local congregation (Acts 14:23; 11:27-30).

3. **The "Mother Church" concept.** Some teach that the elders of larger churches can direct the affairs of smaller churches. The Bible grants no greater authority to any church over another.

4. **"The Pastor" concept.** Some apply the Scriptural name "pastor" to a preacher, and give to this individual sole leadership over the congregation. In some cases this "pastor" is hired and fired by a board of deacons. The Bible always teaches a plurality of elders

(Phil. 1:1). Although a preacher may serve as an elder (1 Tim. 5:17), preachers possess no authority in and of themselves. Deacons, while appointed servants within a church, serve under the authority of the eldership (1 Tim. 3:8-13).

B. The denial of authority.

1. **"Elders have no authority."** In reaction to some of the abuses regarding the authority of the eldership, some have suggested that the elders have no authority. While the authority of the elders is limited to the word of God, the fact that the members are to be submissive and obedient to them makes it clear that they do possess authority (Heb. 13:7, 17).

2 **"There is no such thing as an appointed eldership."** Another reaction to abuse is the claim that the role of elders was limited to the New Testament and their direct appointment by the apostles. While it is clear that the apostles appointed elders (Acts 14:23), they also instructed others to follow their example (Titus 1:5; Phil. 4:9).

> Reaction to abuses of authority has led some to reject the biblical authority given to an eldership.

Conclusion.

The Bible has set elders, bishops, or shepherds over local congregations to lead them in accordance with the dictates of God's word. Although their authority is limited, they do possess the right to lead God's people. In matters of faith, it is the responsibility of every congregation to obey God in all things, even if the eldership does otherwise. In matters of judgment it is the duty of the congregation to submit to the eldership.

Study Questions.

1. Define the Greek word *presbuteros*. What are the two ways it is translated into English? _____

_____

_____

The Eldership of the Church

2. Define the Greek word *episcopos*. What are the two ways it is translated in English? _____

_____

_____

3. Define the Greek word *poimen*. What are the two ways it is translated in English? _____

_____

_____

4. List the two passages where qualifications are given for elders.

a) _____ b) _____

5. List two passages where the responsibilities of elders are addressed.

a) _____ b) _____

6. When members of a congregation submit to the unscriptural guidance of an eldership how does this parallel the Roman Catholic doctrine of "papal infallibility"? _____

_____

_____

_____

7. Explain the concepts of expanded oversight and the "mother-church" concept. How do these ideas conflict with Scripture?

_____

_____

_____

_____

_____

8. In the religious world one of the most common names given to a preacher for a local congregation is "pastor." In Scripture to whom was this term applied? _____

_____

9. Can a preacher be an elder (1 Tim. 5:17)? _____
When this happens how must it be distinct from the "the Pastor" concept? _____

_____

10. What are some things taught in Hebrews 13:7 and 13:17 that show that elders are given authority to lead? _____

_____

_____

Lesson Twelve
The Social Gospel

Introduction.

The historical movement known as the "Social Gospel Movement" involved religious groups shifting their focus away from an emphasis upon the next life and seeking to cure social problems through applying biblical principles. In our own day even among those who still emphasize the next life there is an increasing emphasis upon appealing to man's social needs as a way to motivate interest in spiritual matters. This may involve anything from churches building gymnasiums and playgrounds, to providing medical treatment to those in needy countries. In this lesson we will consider what the Bible teaches about the "Social Gospel."

> Many churches now offer things that appeal to social needs to motivate spiritual interest.

I. How does the Gospel Address Man's Social Needs?

A. Man's nature is both physical and spiritual (Eccl. 12:7; 2 Cor. 4:18; Gal. 5:17; Rom. 5:3-4).

B. A spiritual kingdom exists in a physical world (John 17:6, 14-16; Rom.13:1; Eph. 4:28; 2 Tim. 3:12; Eph. 1:3; Matt. 5:16).

II. What Should Draw People to Christ?

A. How do we understand the Lord's example of benevolence? Why did Jesus practice benevolence?

1. Compassion (Mark 8:1-3; John 6:1, 2, 15; 51-54; Matt. 19:16-22).

2. To confirm personal belief (John 4:46-48, 54).

B. The Social Gospel approach. Today we have churches using benevolence as a "carrot at the end of the stick" trying to draw people by it.

1. This kind of thinking leads to twisted priorities. In some churches that practice this, ladies view it as part of their "duty to Christ" to forsake the assembly so they can be back in the "church kitchen" preparing food for the dinner after services.

> Whatever enticement we use to draw people is what it will take to keep them.

2. N. B. Hardeman is quoted as having said, "The less religion a person has the more fried chicken it takes to keep him interested in church." Whatever enticement we use to draw people is exactly what it takes to keep them.

3. **What drew early believers to Christ?** (Acts 2:41; 1 Thess. 2:13-14; 1 Cor. 9:19-23). It was the message of the gospel.

C. Is it the duty of the Church to help the poor and needy of the world?

1. Although the New Testament church was responsible to assist needy Christians (see Acts 11:27-30; 1 Tim. 5:16), there is no example of the church collectively providing benevolence to non-Christians.

2. As individuals it is the responsibility of Christians to help those around us as we have the means and opportunity (Gal. 6:10).

III. The New Testament Church and Common Meals.

A. Did they eat as a church? (1 Cor. 11:20-22, 33, 34).

1. The Lord's Supper is a memorial, not a meal for hunger.

2. Eating together is not a work of the church.

B. *"What about the 'Love Feasts' of Jude 12?"* "In the pl., *agapai*, love feasts, public banquets of a frugal kind instituted by the early Christian church and connected with the celebration of the Lord's

Supper. The provisions were contributed by the more wealthy individuals and were made common to all Christians, whether rich or poor, who chose to partake. Portions were also sent to the sick and absent members. These love feasts were intended as an exhibition of that mutual love which is required by the Christian faith, but **as they became subject to abuses, they were discontinued**" (*The Complete Word Study Dictionary*, by Spiros Zodiates, 66, emphasis mine).

C. "Doesn't The Word 'Fellowship' Refer To Social Interaction?"

1. **"Fellowship"** refers to joint-participation (1 John 1:1-4).

2. The context determines the activity in which they were jointly participating.

3. The New Testament focuses on joint-participation in the gospel (Phil. 1:5). "Fellowship" doesn't mean eating together.

Conclusion.

> The word "fellowship" refers to spiritual interaction—it does not mean eating together.

Man is a spiritual creature dwelling within a physical body. The focus of the gospel and the primary responsibility of the church is to address man's spiritual needs. There are responsibilities that the church has to assist Christians in need, but it is not the work of the church to attempt to feed, clothe, and provide medical treatment to the world. While Christians as individuals should do all that we can when we see others in need, this is an individual responsibility not the work of the church. In the same way, while Christians are encouraged to spend time with one another outside of the assembly, it is not the work of the church to provide the opportunities for this interaction. Neither is it the role of the church to provide social incentives as a lure to motivate non-believers to obedience to the gospel. The word of the truth of the Gospel is God's means of drawing people to Himself.

Study Questions.

1. What was the aim of the historical "Social Gospel" movement?

The Social Gospel

_____

_____

2. Is the gospel intended to improve man's material or spiritual condition (cf. John 16:33)? _____

_____

3. Is it honest to draw people by one thing when we really want them for a different reason? _____

_____

4. What does John indicate in John 4:46-48, 54 was the motive for Jesus' good deeds and signs? _____

_____

_____

_____

5. In Acts 2:41 what drew people to Christ? _____

_____

6. There is no Biblical example of the church offering benevolence to non-Christians. Who was the subject of the benevolence extended in Acts 11:27-30? _____

_____

_____

7. The term "love feasts" is used only once in Jude 12. It is unclear if it is used metaphorically of Christian interaction, of the Lord's Supper, or even of private gatherings among individual Christians. How does 1 Corinthians 11:34 make it clear that eating together is not an authorized work of the church? _____

_____

_____

8. In 1 John 1:1-2 the apostle declares to the reader the eternal life which is manifested in Jesus. In 1 John 1:3 he explains that he declares this so that in accepting the truth the reader might be in "fellowship" with him—going on to declare that he is in "fellowship" with "the Father and with His Son Jesus Christ." What does this indicate about the nature of "fellowship" in Christ? _____

_____

Lesson Thirteen
Marriage, Divorce, and Remarriage

Introduction.

By current statistics, one out of every two marriages in the United States ends in divorce. Even among religious people the epidemic of infidelity to one's mate and to one's marriage vows has led many in the world to believe that divorce is acceptable to God. What is and is not acceptable to God has never been determined by statistics or popular opinion. It has always been determined by the word of God.

I. God Hates "Putting Away" (Mal. 2:13-17).

A. God declared through Malachi, that He hates the abuse, and treachery that is involved in divorce.

1. From a Biblical standpoint, marriage at its very core is a **"covenant"** that God witnesses and seals for those who have the right to make such a contract with one another (Mal. 2:14).

2. In this covenant, two people pledge to be there for one another, through all that life offers them until death. As a result, a husband or wife is intended to be the only person in the world who shares the whole spectrum of personal experience with their mate. They will smile with one another through the good times, clean and care for each other when they are sick and old, and be closer to one another than anyone else has the right to be. Divorce is the breaking of this covenant.

3. **In Scripture divorce was understood to be an act committed by one mate against another.** The man **"put away"** his wife. Under Mosaic Law, only the man could **"put away"** his wife (Deut. 24:1).

> Marriage is a covenant between a man and woman that establishes a closer bond to each other than any other human relationship.

B. Mosaic law on marriage and divorce should not be seen as Divine approval of "putting away" (Deut. 24:1-4). In fact, it set in place laws restricting and deterring its practice.

1. The man who might callously put away his mate, put her in a situation in which, to survive she would be forced to remarry. When this occurred, the first husband could never take her back (Deut. 24:4). This is not restated under the Law of Christ. Under Christ, reconciliation is possible (1 Cor. 7:11).

II. The Doctrine of Christ on Marriage and Divorce.

A. Jesus taught one man and one woman for life (Matt. 19:1-9).

1. In response to the Pharisees' question, Jesus went back to God's establishment of marriage to show that **"from the beginning"** God intended for marriage to last for life (Matt. 19:6; cf. 1 Cor. 7:39; Rom. 7:2).

B. Jesus' taught that divorce and remarriage (in general) is adultery (Matt. 5:31-32; Mark 10:11-12; Luke 16:18).

> Only two of Jesus' four statements on divorce include the exception. This emphasizes the general prionciple.

1. Of the four times that Jesus addresses marriage and divorce in the gospels, two of the four do not even list the exception for **"sexual immorality."** This shows us that the emphasis of Jesus' teaching is on the permanence of marriage rather than the terms under which it can be dissolved.

2. Scripture never grants the right of remarriage to the one who is **"put away"** (whether guilty of fornication or innocent).

C. The only terms under which remarriage is not considered adultery is when an innocent mate **"puts away"** a guilty mate for **"sexual immorality"** (Matt. 5:32; 19:9).

Marriage, Divorce, and Remarriage

1. This **"sexual immorality"** must be **"the cause"** of the **"putting away."** Jesus is not addressing immorality that occurs after the putting away. In that case **"the cause"** would be something other than **"sexual immorality,"** and the remarriage **"adultery."**

III. Paul's Teaching on Marriage and Divorce.

A. Most of what Paul taught on marriage and divorce was what Jesus had already taught. Paul simply clarified some specifics that Jesus had not addressed while on earth (1 Cor. 7:10-16).

1. This can be seen from Paul's use of the phrases **"not I, but the Lord says"** and **"I, not the Lord, say."** As an inspired writer, even his own statements were **"the commandments of the Lord"** (1 Cor. 14:37).

2. The Greek literally describes circumstances imposed upon a woman (1 Cor. 7:10-11). In other words one who has **"been separated from her husband"** is to remain unmarried or be reconciled, and a husband is not to **"put away"** his wife to begin with. This admonition to remain unmarried is not saying that one can divorce but just **"remain unmarried"** with the Lord's approval. Jesus taught that what God has joined together man is not to separate (Matt. 19:6).

B. Paul's teachings regarding *the departure* **of an unbeliever do not constitute a second exception for remarriage (1 Cor. 7:15).**

1. Paul uses a word that is elsewhere used of slavery. A believer's obligation to his or her unbelieving spouse is not *enslaving* to the extent that if the unbeliever leaves the believer can't be right with the Lord. This does not grant the right of remarriage—but the believer has not sinned when this occurs.

> As an apostle the words Paul wrote were "the commandments of the Lord."

61

Marriage, Divorce, and Remarriage

Conclusion.

God established the covenant of marriage as a beautiful bond between a man and a woman, in order to grant to both, companionship, love, intimacy, and provision within this life. Those who would love God, seek true happiness, and strive for eternal life must honor the covenant of marriage no matter how far the world goes in rejection of God's will.

Study Questions

1. In Malachi's revelation that the Lord "hates divorce" with what does he say that it covers one's garments (Mal. 2:13-17)? What does this mean? _____
_____
_____

2. Many of us have signed contracts that required the presence of a notary to confirm the transaction. When Malachi defines marriage as a "covenant," what role does he indicate that God plays in this transaction (Mal. 2:14)? _____
_____

3. Under Mosaic Law, could a woman "put away" her husband (Deut. 24:1-4)? _____

4. What did the Mosaic Law teach about reconciliation after divorce if a woman had married another man after being "put away" (Deut. 24:2-3)? _____
_____
_____

5. Does the Law of Christ restate this restriction regarding reconciliation (cf. 1 Cor. 7:11)? _____

6. What does Jesus teach was not intended "from the beginning" (Matt. 19:1-9)? _____

Marriage, Divorce, and Remarriage

7. Matthew 19:1-9 and Mark 10:1-12 both record the same encounter Jesus had with the Pharisees, but each adds some details. What element of the Pharisees' question does Matthew record that Mark does not? _____

Could this explain why Matthew records the exception and Mark does not? _____

_____

8. Matthew records a fuller answer to the Pharisees. Where and to whom does Mark record Jesus' answer that simply addresses the basic principle (Mark 10:10-12)? _____

_____

What teaching regarding women does Mark record that Matthew did not (Mark 10:12)? _____

_____

9. In all four of the accounts of Jesus' teaching on remarriage for one who is "put away" how is this remarriage always described (Matt. 5:31-32; 19:9; Mark 10:11-12; Luke 16:18)? _____

_____

> We must honor the covenant of marriage no matter how far the world goes in rejection of God's will.

10. If a couple divorces because of "incompatibility" but then one of them remarries, Jesus defines this remarriage as "adultery" but would "sexual immorality" have been "the cause" of the "putting away" (cf. Matt. 5:31-32 and 19:9)? _____

11. Explain what Paul means when he says "not I, but the Lord says" or "I, not the Lord, say" (1 Cor. 7:10-16; 14:37). _____

_____

_____

12. What two options does Paul offer to the woman who "has been separated from her husband" in 1 Corinthians 7:10-11?

a) _____

b) _____

13. The "bondage" that Paul speaks of in 1 Corinthians 7:15 if an unbeliever "departs" is not a word usually used of marriage. To what does it usually refer? _____

_____

Lesson Fourteen
Premillennialism

Throughout history there have been religious groups that have believed that the promises of Christ reigning for 1000 years, described in Revelation chapter twenty, speak of a coming earthly kingdom. Those who hold to this view, believe that there will be a "rapture" of the saints, sparing them from a period of severe tribulation. This view has led many to interpret ongoing political events in light of this anticipated tribulation and earthly kingdom. In this lesson we will consider what the Bible teaches about these doctrines.

I. The Promises of Revelation Chapter Twenty.

A. The Binding of Satan (Rev. 20:1-3).

1. **Old Testament prophecy associated the restriction of demonic power with the reign of the Messiah** (Zech. 13:1-6).

2. **Jesus described the work of the apostles as conquering Satan** (Luke 10:17-20).

B. The 1000 Year Reign (Rev. 20:4-6).

1. The text speaks of the **"souls"** of those martyred for Christ living with Christ. There is no indication that this **"first resurrection"** is a bodily earthly resurrection.

2. **Nothing is said about Jesus reigning upon the earth.** Before His ascension His universal authority was declared (Matt. 28:18-20).

C. Final Judgment (Rev. 20:7-15).

1. **All opposition to the reign of Christ will be brought to a complete end.** If this passage describes Jesus reigning upon the earth

> There is no indication that Revelation 20:4-6 deals with an earthly resurrection.

Premillennialism

in a future kingdom, will He allow rebellion on the earth while He sits on the throne prior to this final victory?

2. Satan and all who follow him will be cast into the lake of fire (i.e. hell).

3. All will be resurrected and judged. 1 Corinthians 15:20-25 teaches that Christ will deliver the kingdom over to the Father when death is brought to an end.

II. The Nature of the Kingdom.

> The prophecy of Daniel identifies when the Messiah's kingdom would come.

A. The Prophecy of Daniel.

1. The prophet Daniel prophesied that during the third kingdom to reign after Babylon an eternal kingdom would be set up (Dan. 2:28-44).

2. The Roman Empire was the third kingdom to rule after Babylon and Jesus established the church during this reign (Luke 3:1-6).

B. Jesus' statements about the kingdom.

1. Jesus declared that His kingdom was not of this world (John 18:33-38).

2. He declared the kingdom would not come with observation but was within (Luke 17:20-21).

3. Jesus declared that some who were alive then would not die until they saw the kingdom come with power (Mark 9:1).

4. With this Jesus declared plainly that His kingdom is not earthly, observable, or to be established later than the lifetime of some who were alive in the first century.

C. The apostles' statements about the kingdom.

1. Paul told the Colossians that Christ had already translated them into the kingdom (Col. 1:13-14).

2. John spoke of those alive when he lived who were his brothers and companions in the kingdom (Rev. 1:9).

3. It is clear that the very apostle who wrote the promises of the thousand year reign already understood Christ to be reigning over him and others.

III. When Will the Saints Be "Caught Up to Meet Him"? (I Thess. 4:13-5:5).

A. The resurrection and Jesus' coming.

1. When Jesus returns He will bring with Him those who **"sleep in Jesus"** not just the martyrs.

2. When Jesus returns the dead in Christ will rise. This must be what Revelation chapter twenty calls **"the second resurrection."**

B. "Meet the Lord in the air."

> Those who are "caught up" will "always be with the Lord" —not raptured away while He sets up an earthly reign.

1. The saved will **"meet the Lord in the air"** and **"always be with the Lord."** There is no indication that Jesus will return to the earth itself. The heaven and earth will be destroyed at His return (2 Pet. 3:10-13).

2. There is no indication that those **"caught up"** will be separated from Jesus, thus being spared from some tribulation or awaiting an earthly kingdom. Passages that refer to some taken and some left properly refer to either the destruction of Jerusalem and those taken captive or being **"taken"** in judgment not to some pre-kingdom rapture (cf. Matt. 24:40-41 and Luke 21:20-24.)

Premillennialism

Conclusion.

The Bible teaches that Jesus established His kingdom when He came to this earth and was exalted as King. The Bible teaches that the church is Christ's kingdom. The Bible promises that when Jesus returns He will bring the resurrection and the final judgment. Living saints will be **"caught up"** to meet Jesus in the air, but the end of this world will come when this takes place.

Study Questions.

1. We observed in lesson seven the prophecy of Zechariah 13:1-6 regarding "the prophet." What does it also promise regarding "the evil spirit"? _____
How might this relate to the prophecy of Revelation 20:1-3?
_____
_____
_____

2. In Revelation 20:4-6 of whom is it said that they "lived and reigned with Christ"? _____
Does anything in the text demand that we understand this of a bodily resurrection on earth? _____

3. What does 1 Corinthians 15:20-25 promise will happen when Jesus returns? _____

4. Much of the misconception of Premillennialism rest on a misunderstanding of the nature of Christ's kingdom. When does the prophecy of Daniel place the coming of the Messiah's eternal kingdom (Dan. 2:28-44)? _____
_____
_____
Has this time period already come (cf. Luke 3:1-6)? _____

5. What did Jesus tell Pilate regarding an earthly kingdom (John 18:33-38)? _____

Premillennialism

_____

_____

6. According to Jesus, would the coming of His kingdom be an observable event (Luke 17:20-21)? _____
   If an early kingdom was set up in Jerusalem, wouldn't that be observable? _____

7. Who would still be alive when the kingdom was to come (Mark 9:1)?

   _____

8. Who does Paul tell the Colossians was already in the kingdom (Col. 1:13-14)? _____

   _____

9. The apostle John is the one who wrote the prophecy of Revelation 20:1-6 regarding a 1000 year reign. Did he teach that the kingdom already existed in the first century (Rev. 1:9)? _____

10. According to 1 Thessalonians 4:13-5:5 who will Christ bring with Him when He returns? _____

    _____

11. Those who teach a pre-tribulation rapture argue that the saved will be spared this tribulation when they are "caught up." With whom does 1 Thessalonians 4:13-5:5 promise the saved will be when Jesus returns?

    _____

    Does this text say anything about an earthly reign? _____

12. What does 2 Peter 3:10-13 promise will burn up when Jesus returns?

    _____

    _____

13. To what do statements about being "taken" or "left" properly refer?

    _____

    _____

    _____

14. If the righteous are taken away during a period of tribulation, who would remain to fight with Jesus in an imagined global war to establish Christ's kingdom? _____

    _____

    _____

Credits

Cover Photo: Composite photo – Kyle Pope from public domain images • Page 3 Composite photo – Kyle Pope from public domain images • Page 5: Composite photo – Kyle Pope from public domain images • Page 7: Man reading in front of blinds photo – *Key Photos for Windows and Macintosh CD* • Page 8: Bible photo – public domain • Page 9: Composite photo – Kyle Pope from public domain images • Page 11: Man reading by boat photo – *PhotoDisc Starter Kit CD* • Page 13: Bible photo – public domain • Page 14: Composite photo – Kyle Pope from public domain images • Page 16: Composite cross photo – Kyle Pope from public domain images • Page 18: Bible photo – public domain • Page 19: Composite photo – Kyle Pope from public domain images • Page 22: Bible photo – public domain • Page 23: Composite photo – Kyle Pope from public domain images • Page 24: Baptistery – Kyle Pope • Page 26: Bible photo – public domain • Page 27: Composite photo – Kyle Pope from public domain images • Page 28: Guitar player photo – *PhotoDisc Starter Kit CD* • Page 31: Bible photo – public domain • Page 32: Composite photo – Kyle Pope from public domain images • Page 34: Dove photo – public domain • Page 36: Bible photo – public domain • Page 37: Composite photo – Kyle Pope from public domain images • Page 38: Communion tray – Kyle Pope • Page 40: Bible photo – public domain • Page 41: Composite photo – Kyle Pope from public domain images • Page 44: Bible photo – public domain • Page 45: Composite photo – Kyle Pope from public domain images • Page 46: Woman reading – *PhotoDisc Starter Kit CD* • Page 49: Bible photo – public domain • Page 51: Composite photo – Kyle Pope from public domain images • Page 52: Apostle photo – public domain • Page 54: Bible photo – public domain • Page 55: Composite photo – Kyle Pope from public domain images • Page 56: Potluck photo – Public domain • Page 58: Bible photo – public domain • Page 59: Composite photo – Kyle Pope from public domain images • Page 60: Wedding ring photo – *Expert Software, Photo CD Gallery No. 2* • Page 62: Bible photo – public domain • Page 64: Composite photo – Kyle Pope from public domain images • Page 65: Jerusalem photo – Kyle Pope • Page 68: Bible photo – public domain • Back Cover Photo: Composite photo – Kyle Pope from public domain images.

CPSIA information can be obtained at www.ICGtesting.com
Printed in the USA
BVOW04s0647180816

459141BV00003B/9/P

9 781584 273868